What's Living in Your Bedroom?

Andrew Solway

Heinemann Library
Chicago, Illinois

302208184
L

Customer Service 888-454-2279
Visit our website at www.heinemannlibrary.com

Designed by David Poole and Paul Myerscough
Illustrations: Geoff Ward
Originated by Dot Gradations
Printed and bound in China by South China Printing Company

08 07 06 05 04
10 9 8 7 6 5 4 3 2 1

Library of Congress Cataloging-in-Publication Data
Solway, Andrew.
 What's living in your bedroom? / Andrew Solway.
   v. cm. -- (Hidden life)
Contents: Taking a closer look -- Specks of dust -- Dust busters -- Living
dust -- Airborne illness -- Bed bugs -- More blood-suckers -- Carpet
crawlers -- Clothes moths -- Chewing old wood -- Moldy and rotten --
Passengers and parasites.
  ISBN 1-4034-4845-0 (hc : lib. bdg.) -- ISBN 1-4034-5484-1 (pc)
 1. Bedrooms--Microbiology--Juvenile literature. 2. Housing and
health--Juvenile literature. [1. Microbiology. 2. Housing and health.]
I.
Title. II. Series.
QR100.S65 2004
579'.17554--dc22

                         2003018006

Acknowledgments
The author and publishers are grateful to the following for permission to reproduce copyright material: p. 4 Alamy Images; p. 5t Science Photo Library (R. Maisonneuve, Publiphoto Diffusion), pp. 5b, 22 (Astrid and Hanns Freider Michler), pp. 6-7 (Medical Stock Photo), pp. 6b, 14, 19 (David Scharf), p. 7b (Tony and Daphne Hallas), p. 8 (Alfred Pasieka), p. 10t (Andy Harmer), p. 10b (Dr Karl Lounatmaa), p. 11 (Lee D. Simon), p. 12 (Chris Priest and Mark Clarke), p. 13L (Linda Steinmark Custom Medical Stock Photo), p. 13r (A.B. Dowsett), p. 15t (Sinclair Stammers), p. 16 (John Burbridge), p. 17 (K.H. Kjeldsen), 24r (Vaughan Fleming), p. 24b (Sidney Moulds), p. 25t (E. Gueho), p. 27t (Pascal Goetgheluck), p. 26 (Andrew Syred) p. 27b (Eye of Science); p. 9 Corbis (Tom Stewart), p. 15b (Kelly Mooney Photography); p. 20t Holt Studio International; pp. 18, 23t Oxford Scientific Films; p. 20b Oxford Scientific Films (Mike Birkhead), p. 23b (Frank Schneidermeyer); p. 21 Tudor Photography.

Cover photograph of a bedbug reproduced with permission of Science Photo Library/Eye of Science.

Our thanks to Dr. Philip Parrillo, entomologist at the Field Museum in Chicago, for his comments in the preparation of this book.

Some words are shown in bold, **like this.** You can find out what they mean by looking in the glossary.

Contents

Many of the photos in this book were taken using a microscope.
In the captions you may see a number that tells you how much
they have been enlarged. For example, a photo marked "(x200)"
is about 200 times bigger than in real life.

Taking a Closer Look

A bedroom is not the kind of place you expect to find a lot of life. All animals need food, so unless you have regular midnight feasts, there are not many leftovers for pests such as mice and cockroaches. But if you could take a look around your bedroom with a microscope, you might be surprised at what you would find.

A bedroom does not contain much of what we would call food, but some tiny creatures eat strange stuff. How would you like to eat skin flakes instead of cornflakes? Or perhaps you would prefer chewing on your clothes or on some wood? Living in your bedroom are creatures that eat all these things.

This bedroom looks empty of all living things. But if you could look closer, you would find a lot of hidden life.

Bugs in the bed

Your bed is one place where you can find hidden life. At night it is warm, and there is a very good source of food—you! Another place that tiny bugs like to live is in the carpet. You might also find some in your closet snacking on old clothes.

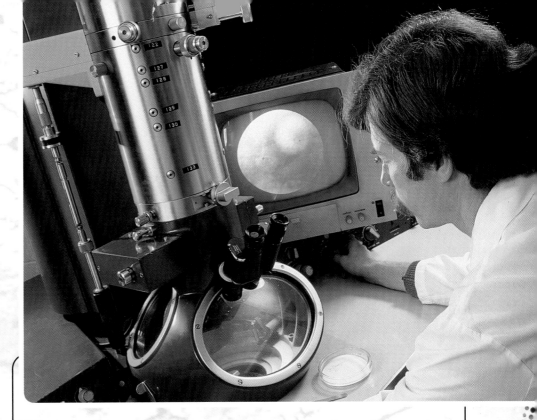

Electron microscopes *are expensive and complicated to use. To look at creatures under an electron microscope, they have to be killed.*

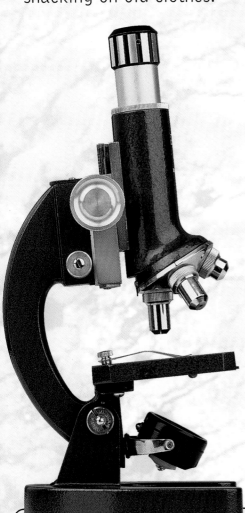

Light microscopes are easy to use, and they can be used to look at living creatures.

Microbes

If you turn up the power on your microscope, you will find many tiny **microbes** around the bedroom. Microbes live on your skin, so whenever you touch something, you leave some of these microbes behind. Microbes even float around with the dust in the air. Every time you breathe in, some of these microbes get into your nose and throat.

MICROSCOPES

The reason we know so much about the hidden life around us is because scientists have used microscopes to study microbes. A light microscope—the kind of microscope that you might have used at school or at home—can magnify things up to 1,800 times. But to get a close look at really tiny microbes such as bacteria, you need an electron microscope. This can magnify objects up to 500,000 times.

Specks of Dust

When the sun comes in through your bedroom window, you might see golden specks dancing in the sunbeams. These specks are dust. Under a microscope, a speck of dust becomes a mixture of all kinds of things.

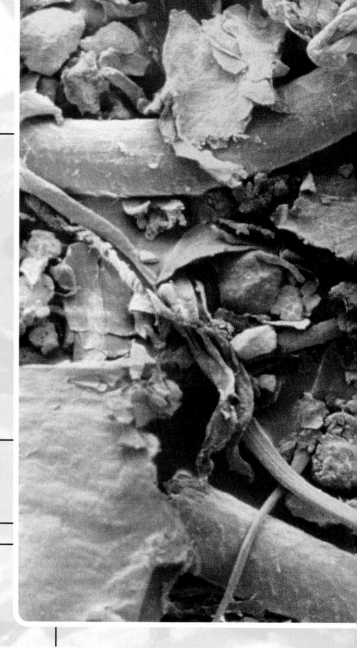

This sample of household dust contains clothing fibers, pet hairs, and flakes of human skin.

Pollen grains often have beautiful, elaborate shapes (x1310). Their shape may help them to float on the slightest current of air.

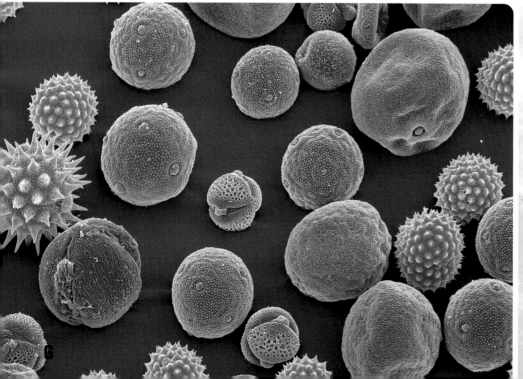

What do you think dust is made of? Bits of rock perhaps, or soil? In fact, it is neither of these things. The most common thing in household dust is skin. The outer layers of our skin are made of dead **cells.** We are constantly shedding tiny bits of this dead skin. New skin grows below the surface to replace the skin we shed.

Dust is so complex a mixture that the dust from a particular place is different from the dust from anywhere else. Scientists who help solve crimes study the many types of dust and can use the information in dust to connect a criminal to the scene of a crime.

These streaks of light in the night sky are meteors—small pieces of rock that burn up as they enter the **atmosphere.** They add to the dust found on Earth.

An amazing mixture

Household dust is a mixture of an amazing number of things. In addition to skin there is hair, fibers from clothing, the droppings of insects and other tiny creatures, and living things such as **pollen** from plants, **bacteria,** and other **microbes.**

COSMIC DUST

Some of the dust particles in your house may be visitors from outer space. Every day, large and small rocks from outer space hit the Earth as it travels around the sun. Most of these rocks break up into tiny dust particles as they fall through the atmosphere. About 40,000 tons of space dust falls to Earth each year. This is a tiny amount compared to the total amount of dust in the air, but there are probably a few specks of space dust mixed in with the other dust in your bedroom.

Dust Busters

Wherever there is dust, you are likely to find dust mites. These tiny creatures are not insects, but eight-legged relatives of spiders. Dust mites can live in your mattress, your pillows, or the carpet without you ever knowing they are there. But if you suffer from **asthma,** they may be a problem.

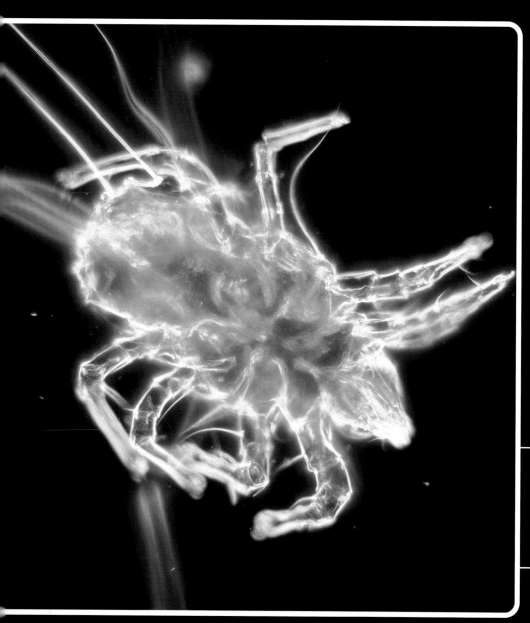

Dust mites are about 0.008 inch (0.2 mm) long. They have no eyes, but the long hairs on their bodies are sensitive to touch and help them find their way around. Dust mites are **scavengers** that live on whatever food they can find. One of the main things they eat is flakes of skin. They also eat **fungi, pollen,** parts of dead insects, and other such tasty-sounding food.

Dust mites are partly see-through, which makes them very difficult to see (x188).

Mites in the millions

You won't believe how many dust mites there could be in your bedroom. A pillow may contain thousands of mites, while 10 million mites could be living in your mattress.

The amount of dust in your bedroom will affect the numbers of dust mites. But dust mites like warm, wet conditions, and the conditions in your bedroom are more important than the amount of dust. A house in a warm, wet **climate** will have more mites than a house in a dry, cold place.

How mites live

A dust mite begins life as an egg, which hatches after a few days into a **larva.** The larva eats the same food as an adult. Once it reaches a certain size, the larva **molts** (sheds its skin) twice, passing through two **nymph** stages. After eating and growing for a time, it molts again to become an adult.

Soon after the adult mites mate, the male dies. The female mites lay 40 to 100 eggs over a period of two months.

Mite allergy

Although mites themselves do us no harm, their droppings become part of household dust, and for some people this can be a problem. Many people are **allergic** to dust mite droppings, and this can cause symptoms such as sneezing, red eyes, and a runny nose. In some people it can trigger an attack of **asthma.**

Modern vacuum cleaners now come equipped with filters small enough to capture dust mite droppings. Older models would simply blow clouds of these tiny particles all over the room.

Living Dust

As we have seen, living things are part of the dust in the air. **Microbes** may float freely in the air, or they may be part of bigger dust specks or droplets of liquid.

Earth star is a type of fungus that grows in forests. This earth star is releasing a cloud of spores.

*When a bacterium forms a spore, the **nucleus** of the cell is surrounded by a tough coating with several layers (x57,456).*

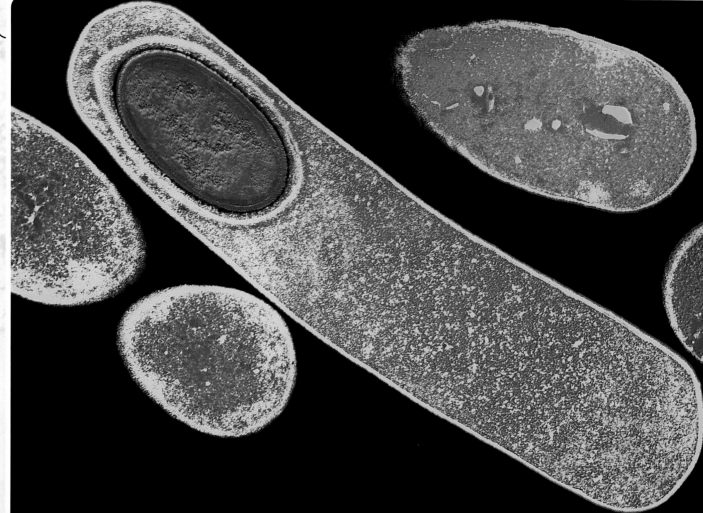

Bacteria

Bacteria are tiny, simple living things, each one just a single **cell.** They are small enough to float on the slightest breeze. However, bacteria dry out quickly in the air, so they have to be protected when they are **airborne.** Some bacteria survive because they are inside tiny water droplets. Others form a thick-coated **spore** when they find themselves in harsh conditions. Inside this spore, the bacterium can survive drying out, low and high temperatures, and harmful chemicals. If and when conditions improve, a new bacterium grows from the spore.

Fungi

Fungi are neither plants nor animals. Most fungi either grow on dead or rotting material, or they are **parasites.**

Fungi reproduce by making spores. These are not like bacterial spores. They are like a fungus's seeds. Each fungus produces thousands or millions of very small,

light spores, and often they are released into the air to spread on the wind.

Viruses

The tiniest living particles in the air are **viruses.** Viruses are made up of an outer layer called the coat and an inner layer of **DNA.** A virus cannot move, eat, or reproduce by itself. But if it comes into contact with the right kind of living cell, it infects the cell and uses it to make copies of itself. Some viruses cannot survive outside a living thing for very long, but others can survive for long periods in the air.

The strange shapes on this Escherichia coli *bacterium are T2 phages—viruses that infect bacterial cells (x138,040).*

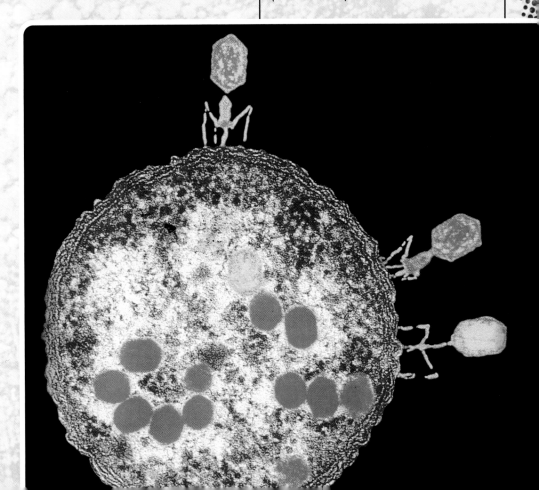

Airborne Illnesses

At some time you probably have had a few days off school with a bad cold or flu, lying in bed coughing, sneezing, and feeling miserable. When you are sick in bed, always make sure you use a tissue when you cough or sneeze. Otherwise you will spread around **microbes** that could easily infect someone else.

> In many countries babies are **vaccinated** against whooping cough. The vaccine protects them against the disease.

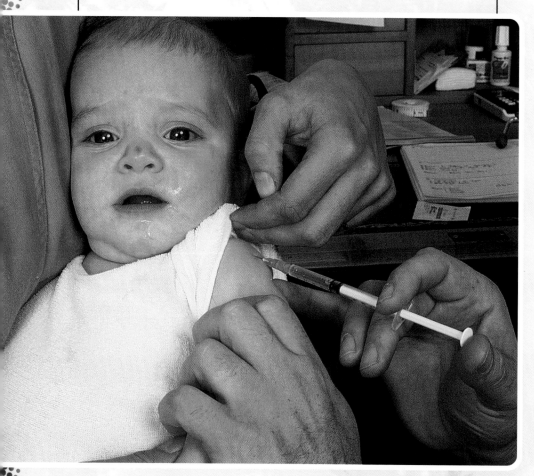

Some microbes in the air can cause disease. Colds, flu, whooping cough, and tuberculosis are just some of the diseases caused by **airborne** microbes. These airborne diseases are often passed on by coughing and sneezing.

How airborne diseases spread

When you cough or sneeze, millions of tiny liquid droplets shoot out of your nose and mouth. If you have a cold, flu, or other airborne disease, some of the droplets contain disease microbes. If someone else breathes in some of the droplets, the microbes get into their body and they may get the disease.

Colds and flu

Illnesses such as colds and flu are caused by **viruses.** Colds are caused by a group of very tiny viruses called rhinoviruses that infect the nose (rhinovirus

When you cough and sneeze a cloud of tiny droplets shoots out into the air.

means "nose virus").
Flu viruses are much bigger than rhinoviruses. They attack the nose, throat, and lungs.

We have some cold and flu viruses in the nose and throat most of the time. But if we breathe in a type of cold or flu virus that our body has not met before, we get ill. After a time, the body builds up a **resistance** to the new virus, and we recover.

Whooping cough

Whooping cough is a disease caused by a tiny **bacterium** called *Bordetella pertussis*. This bacterium infects the **cells** that line the throat. It causes nasty bouts of coughing that end in a "whoop" sound as the person struggles to breathe in.

Mycobacterium tuberculosis *is the bacterium that causes tuberculosis.*

TUBERCULOSIS

The most important bacterial disease passed through the air is tuberculosis (TB). It is caused by bacteria. TB kills 2 million people in the world every year. It is most common in poor countries because the disease often affects people who do not get enough good food or are not healthy enough to fight off disease.

Bedbugs

The biggest item of food in your bedroom is you!
We have seen already how dust mites live off bits of
skin that you shed. But there may also be other bugs
in your bedroom that feed on you at night.

Bedbugs are like tiny vampires. These small, brown,
flattened insects are big enough to see, but they stay
well hidden. During the day they hide either under
the mattress or in cracks around the room. At night
they creep into your bed and take a meal of blood
while you sleep.

Built for bloodsucking

Bedbugs are well adapted
for their bloodsucking
lifestyle. Their flattened
bodies make it easy for
them to squeeze into tiny
cracks and gaps where they
can hide during the day.

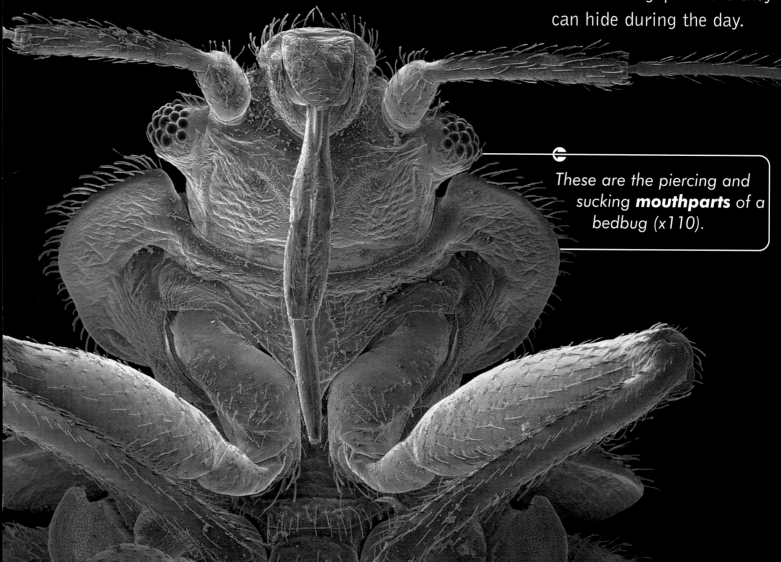

*These are the piercing and
sucking **mouthparts** of a
bedbug (x110).*

Bedbugs use their needlelike **mouthparts** to pierce human skin. Before beginning to suck blood, the bug injects saliva (spit) into the wound. Chemicals in the saliva keep the blood flowing while the bug is eating. Soon the bedbug is completely full of blood and crawls away to digest its meal.

People rarely wake when they are bitten by bedbugs, but the next day they have sore, itchy bites.

From egg to adult
A female bedbug can lay about 200 eggs, in the mattress or in cracks in the walls and floor. Eggs take from one to four weeks to hatch, depending on the temperature. The **nymphs** that hatch from the eggs

🔹 *Bedbugs feed on a human.*

look like the adults, except that they are much smaller and white. A nymph **molts** five times before it becomes an adult, and it must eat at least one blood meal between each molt.

Preventing bedbugs
Bedbugs were a common pest until the middle of the 1900s, but they are much less common today. If you change your sheets regularly and vacuum your bedroom, bedbugs are unlikely to be a problem.

It is often possible to sleep soundly while bedbugs feed on you at night.

More Bloodsuckers

Bedbugs are not the only bloodsucking insects that can be found in bedrooms. If you have pets in the house, there may be fleas in the carpet.

Fleas are bloodsucking insects 0.08 to 0.1 inch (2 to 3 mm) long. There are many different kinds, each of which prefers to feed on a particular kind of animal. The flea most likely to find its way into your bedroom is the cat flea. These fleas live on cats and dogs. But they will also suck blood from a human, leaving a sore, itchy bite.

What fleas are like

Fleas are wingless, brown insects with a small head. They are thin rather than flat, to help them slip between the hairs or feathers on an animal's body.

A flea has no wings, but it has an amazing jump. A flea's jumping ability helps it to move around in search of a **host** and to hitch a ride on a passing animal.

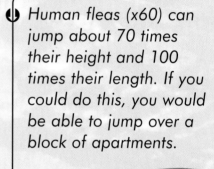

Human fleas (x60) can jump about 70 times their height and 100 times their length. If you could do this, you would be able to jump over a block of apartments.

Eggs and young

You are more likely to find adult fleas on your pet than in the carpet, but pets that have fleas leave eggs behind wherever they go. Flea eggs in the carpet take between two and twelve days to hatch into wormlike **larvae.** The larvae find enough bits of food in the carpet to survive and grow. After two **molts,** they spin **cocoons.**

A flea can stay in its cocoon for up to a year. While inside the cocoon it cannot be killed by **pesticides,** which is why it is often difficult to get rid of fleas. When conditions are good, an adult flea breaks out of the cocoon.

Cat flea larvae are coiled around the fibers in a carpet.

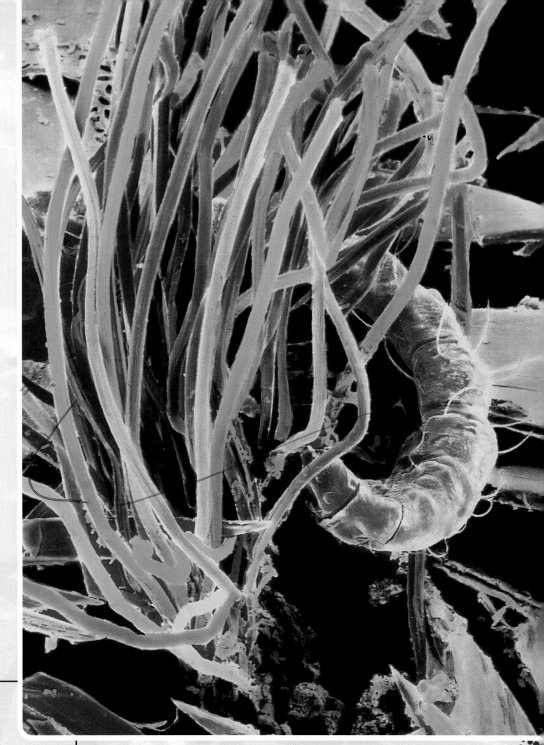

PEOPLE FLEAS

Another kind of flea is specially designed for living on humans. These fleas are quite rare today because they prefer to live on unwashed bodies and hide in dirty clothing. The best place to find human fleas today is in a pigsty! Pigs have a similar biology to humans, and pigsties sometimes get infested with these fleas.

Carpet Crawlers

Is there a trunk of old clothes in your bedroom? Do you have a dresser or closet with old clothes in it? These are the kinds of places you will find carpet beetle **larvae.** These hairy creatures eat things like carpets, woolens, and furniture coverings.

Carpet beetles are common, but unless you get a large **infestation** you will not know they are there. Adult carpet beetles are small, rounded beetles about 0.08 to 0.2 inch (2 to 5 mm) long. They are often black, but sometimes they have orange or yellow markings. The larvae are carrot-shaped and covered in bristles, with a tuft of especially long bristles on the tail.

Pollen feeders

Adult carpet beetles do not live in houses at all. They live outside and eat flower **pollen.**

When a female carpet beetle has **mated,** she looks for somewhere to lay her eggs. Some carpet beetles

➊ *A carpet beetle larva tunnels its way through a carpet.*

A *carpet beetle larva* (x240) has a hairy head.

lay their eggs in the nests of birds, small animals, or insects. However, some find their way into houses and lay their eggs there. One female can lay up to 100 eggs.

Adult carpet beetles like the light, but their larvae prefer dark places. They eat and rest under furniture, in dark corners, or in folds in cloth. Larvae prefer products made from animals, such as wool carpets, fur, or hairs, but they will also eat cotton.

Larvae grow quite slowly. In warm places they take several months to reach full size, but in cooler conditions they can take as long as three years. Once the larva is fully grown, it forms a hard case around itself and becomes a **pupa.** When the adult beetle hatches from the pupa, it flies out of the house.

Keeping out carpet beetles

If you vacuum your bedroom regularly and make sure to do all around the edges and under the furniture, you are unlikely to get carpet beetle larvae. Make sure clothes are clean before you put them away in a closet, wardrobe, chest, or dresser.

Clothes Moths

If something is a bit battered and worse for wear, people sometimes say it looks moth-eaten. Clothes moths are not as common as they were in the past, but they still occasionally invade people's homes and eat holes in their clothes.

A case-making clothes moth caterpillar. Only the head end of the caterpillar sticks out of its case.

These adult clothes moths are on a sweater. Female moths rarely fly, but scurry around instead.

If you notice tiny holes in your clothes and white threads on the surface, then you may have clothes moths. They are very small, dull-colored moths that live in dark, enclosed places such as closets or storage chests. Adult clothes moths do not eat at all. They live only long enough to **mate** and lay eggs. But their caterpillars eat clothing, paper, fur, and other materials.

Silk webs and cases

There are two kinds of clothes moths, and their caterpillars live differently. One kind spins mats or tunnels of silk as they move around. These mats may incorporate caterpillar droppings, so they make clothes messy.

The other kind of caterpillar spins itself a silk case. When it is eating or moving, the front part of the caterpillar sticks out of the case. This case-making caterpillar eats neat, round holes in our clothes.

Hatching

Female clothes moths lay up to 150 eggs, which take between four days and three weeks to hatch. The **larvae** eat until they are full grown, and then they become **pupae.** The case-making kind of caterpillar turns its silk case into a hard **cocoon.** Inside the cocoon the caterpillar turns into an adult moth.

Mothballing clothes

The best way to avoid clothes moths is to wash clothes before storing them and to put them in airtight containers. Dried lavender, cloves, lemon peels, and cedar chips are all good-smelling items that can be put into closets and chests where clothes are stored to keep clothes moths away. Mothballs are small balls made of chemicals that are designed to keep moths away. But they can damage some clothing, and clothes that have been stored with mothballs need airing or cleaning before they can be worn again.

If you store your clean clothes carefully in a dry, airtight closet, you can avoid getting clothes moths.

Chewing Old Wood

Eating old clothes and fur is bad enough, but many kinds of insect **larvae** eat wood. If you have an old house with wooden beams or old furniture in your bedroom, it might have woodworms. Woodworms are the larvae of certain kinds of beetles. They spend years eating tunnels through pieces of wood and then eventually emerge into the light to live for a brief time as adults.

Furniture beetles

The most common types of woodworms are the larvae of furniture beetles. Adult furniture beetles appear in spring and early summer. They fly around looking for a **mate.** After mating, the female lays about 30 eggs in holes or cracks in wood. As soon as the larvae hatch from the eggs, they begin to burrow into the wood. They live in the wood for several years, slowly growing bigger.

When the larvae are fully grown, they work their way back to the surface of the wood. Just below the surface, each larva digs out a small chamber where it turns into a **pupa.** After a few weeks, a new adult beetle emerges from the pupa, bites its way out of the wood, and flies away.

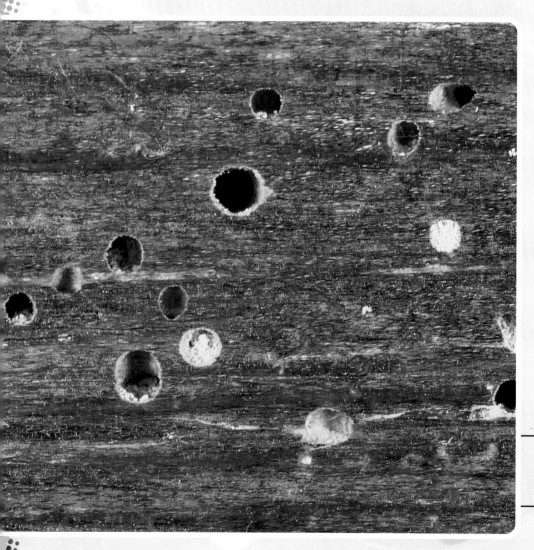

Tunnels made by woodworms can seriously weaken wood.

The death-watch beetle is bigger than the furniture beetle, and it cannot fly.

Death-watch beetles

Another kind of woodworm, found particularly in Great Britain, is known as the death-watch beetle. Death-watch beetles are often found in old churches. When a beetle is looking for a mate, it sends out a signal by tapping on the wood with its head. It is this tapping that gives the death-watch beetle its name. In the past, people hearing the tapping thought it was the tapping of Death coming to claim a victim!

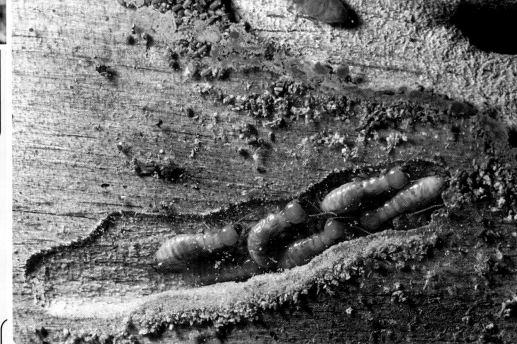

Termites are very destructive.

TROPICAL TERRORS

In tropical countries, the worst pest of wood is the termite. Millions of termites live together in large nests. Wood is their main food, and if they get into the roof beams of a building they can destroy them in a short time. Metal, stone, or cement boards are sometimes fitted around the outside of houses to keep termites out.

Moldy and Rotten

Do you sometimes take a banana to your bedroom and then forget to throw away the peel? Or perhaps you sometimes find an old apple core under the bed? Old banana peels get black and moldy, while apple cores get brown and rotten. Both the mold and the rot are caused by **fungi.**

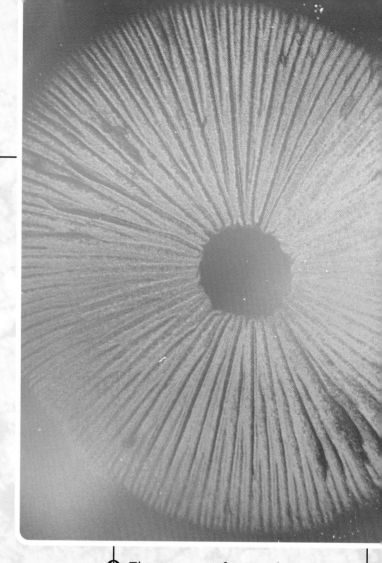

The spores of a mushroom are on the gills that cover the underside of the cap. If you leave the cap of a mushroom on a piece of paper overnight, you get a spore print like this when the spores fall from the gills.

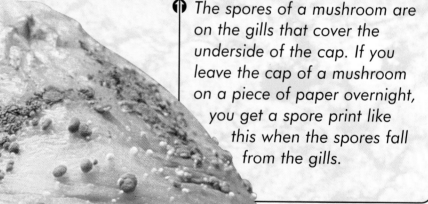

The brown lumps on this apple are caused by the fungus Penicillium.

The best known types of fungi are mushrooms. But what we call mushrooms are not the main mushroom fungus at all. They are structures for producing **spores** (seeds). The body of the mushroom fungus is a mass of incredibly thin threads called **hyphae,** which grow hidden beneath the ground.

Invading threads

The mold fungi that grow on apples, bananas, and other fruits are also made up of masses of hyphae. These tiny fungus threads invade the fruit. A fungus has no mouth or **digestive system.** It simply soaks up its food. To get food from the fruit, it releases chemicals that break it down into simple **nutrients** that the fungus can soak up. These chemicals cause the flesh of a rotting apple to turn almost liquid.

Producing spores

Once a mold has begun to grow and spread, it makes millions of powdery spores. The spores are the seeds that will allow the fungus to spread and grow elsewhere. Bunches of spores grow on tiny stalks, and as they ripen they are released into the air. The spores are light enough to be carried by the slightest current of air.

Releasing poisons

When an apple rots, it is quite easy to scrape off the rotten part and eat the rest. But eating moldy food is not a good idea. In addition to the chemicals they release to digest their food, many molds produce poisons. These poisons can spread through the fruit, beyond the area of the mold growth, and make you very ill.

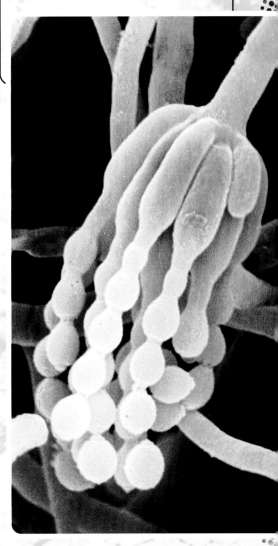

A magnified view (x1210) of the tiny spores of the Penicillium fungus.

Passengers and Parasites

Woodworms, clothes moths, carpet beetles, and many other kinds of insects often have their own, even smaller passengers. They are mites, relatives of the dust mites that live in the carpet. Some kinds are hitchhikers that use insects as air transportation. Others are **scavengers** or **parasites.**

Tiny hitchhikers

Any insects that get into your bedroom are likely to be carrying tiny mite hitchhikers with them. Mites cannot fly, so when, for instance, some young plant-eating mites want to get away from their home plant, they hitch a ride.

Mites hitch a ride on the legs of a beetle (x64).

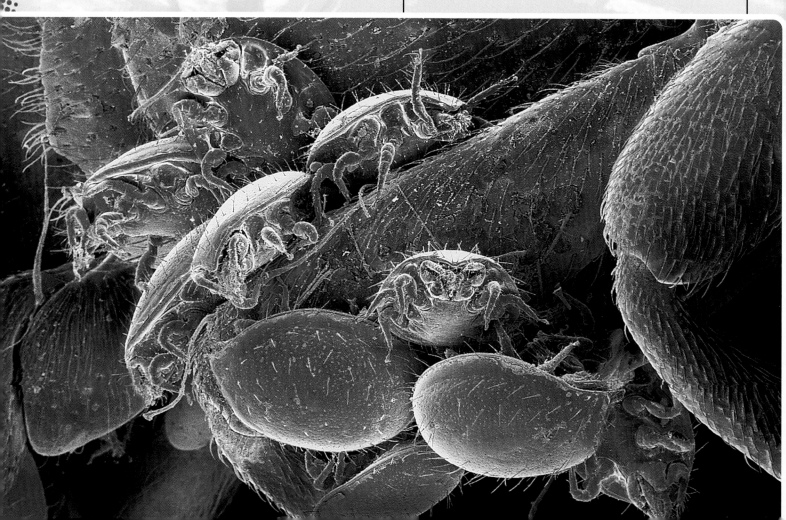

Scavenger mites

Some mites spend most of their time on a particular type of insect, but they do not feed on the insect. Instead, they are scavengers, eating up bits of food that the insect leaves behind, or eat **fungi** that live in the insect's nest. Beetles are often the **hosts** of scavenger mites.

Parasites

Woodworms would seem to have an easy life, protected from **predators** and with a plentiful food supply. But they do have enemies—parasitic mites. These mites live on the woodworm and feed on its body. Because woodworms take so long to grow, there is time for the mites to reproduce. Often mite numbers become so great that they kill their host.

There are many different parasitic mites found on insects. Two of the best known are parasites of honey bees. One very tiny

A grain mite feeds on fungus. Fungus-feeding mites often carry their own hitchhikers: pieces of fungus or fungus **spores.**

kind called *Acarapis woodi* lives its whole life in a honey bee's breathing tubes. At first these mites do not greatly bother the bee, but heavy mite **infestations** can weaken or kill a whole bee **colony.**

The other honey bee mite is the *Varroa* mite. This mite is bigger and lives on the outside of the bee. *Varroa* mites often kill their hosts. In recent years, *Varroa* mites that are resistant to **pesticides** have become a huge problem for beekeepers.

Varroa *mites cling to a honey bee (x74).*

Table of Sizes

Although all hidden life is tiny, there is a huge range of sizes. To a flea, a grain of pollen seems just as tiny as the flea seems to us.

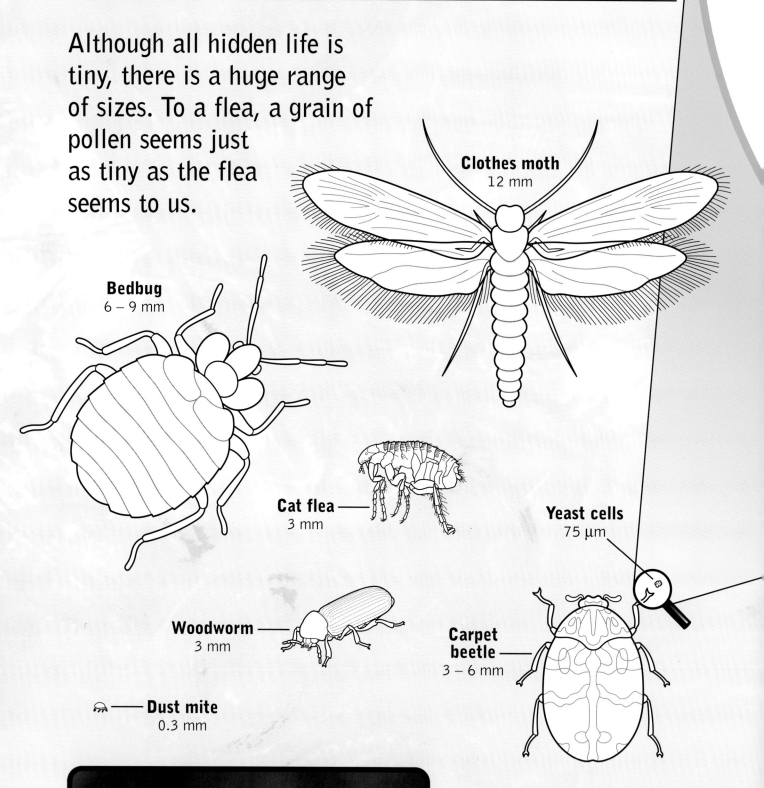

Clothes moth
12 mm

Bedbug
6 – 9 mm

Cat flea —
3 mm

Yeast cells
75 µm

Woodworm —
3 mm

Carpet beetle —
3 – 6 mm

🐜 — **Dust mite**
0.3 mm

HOW SMALL?

1 m (meter) = 1,000 mm (millimeters)
1 mm (millimeter) = 1,000 µm (micrometers)
1 µm (micrometer) = 1,000 nm (nanometers)

These organisms are 10 times bigger than normal.

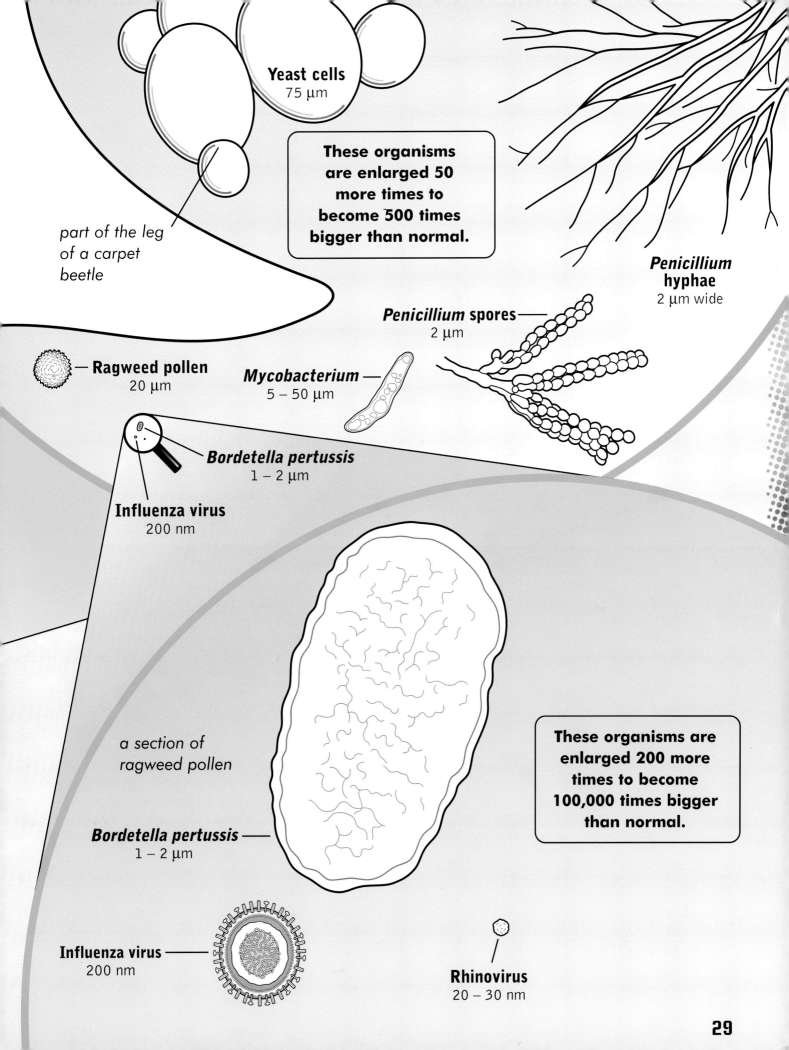

Yeast cells
75 μm

part of the leg
of a carpet
beetle

These organisms
are enlarged 50
more times to
become 500 times
bigger than normal.

Penicillium
hyphae
2 μm wide

Penicillium spores
2 μm

Ragweed pollen
20 μm

Mycobacterium
5 – 50 μm

Bordetella pertussis
1 – 2 μm

Influenza virus
200 nm

a section of
ragweed pollen

These organisms are
enlarged 200 more
times to become
100,000 times bigger
than normal.

Bordetella pertussis
1 – 2 μm

Influenza virus
200 nm

Rhinovirus
20 – 30 nm

Glossary

airborne carried in the air

allergy condition in which the body overreacts to something that is breathed in, eaten, or gets on the skin. It can cause sneezing, rash, or sickness.

asthma disease of the lungs that causes wheezing and other breathing difficulties

atmosphere the air around us

bacteria microscopic living things, each one only a single cell. They are different from other one-celled creatures because they do not have a nucleus. Only one of these living things is called a bacterium.

cells building blocks of living things. Some living things are single cells, while others are made up of billions of cells working together.

climate usual weather of a region

cocoon silky, cigar-shaped case spun by many insect larvae to protect them while they change from larvae into adults

colony group of creatures of one kind living close together

digestive system group of organs in animals that break down food into nutrients that the body can absorb and use for energy. It includes the stomach, intestines, and other organs.

DNA material that makes up the genes of living cells

electron microscope very powerful microscope that can magnify objects up to 500,000 times

fungus plantlike living thing such as a mushroom or a yeast. Two or more of these organisms are called fungi.

host animal or plant that a parasite lives on

hyphae thin, threadlike cells that make up the body of most fungi. Only one of these cells is called a hypha.

infestation when something is overrun with a harmful or irritating creature such as an insect

larva the young stage of some types of insects. A larva looks different from an adult and has to go through a changing stage (the pupa) in order to become an adult.

mate when a male and female animal get together to reproduce

microbe microscopic creature such as a bacterium, protozoan, fungus, or virus

molt to shed skin, feathers, or hair

mouthparts jaws or other parts that an insect uses to take in food

nucleus round structure surrounded by a membrane, found inside a living cell. It contains the cell's genes.

nutrient chemical that nourishes living things

nymph the young of some types of insects and mites. Nymphs usually look similar to their parents and change gradually into adults during several molts.

parasite creature that lives on or in another living creature and takes its food, without giving any benefit in return and sometimes causing harm

pesticide chemicals that are used to kill insects or other animals that are pests, for instance those that cause disease or eat crops

pollen fine powder produced by flowers to fertilize other flowers

predator animal that hunts and kills other animals for food

pupa a stage in the growth of an insect in which the insect changes from a larva into an adult. More than one pupa are called pupae.

resistance body's ability to fight off disease

scavenger animal that feeds on dead or waste material

spore very tiny seedlike structure that a fungus uses to reproduce. A bacterial spore is a bacterium that has formed a tough outer coat to help it survive difficult conditions.

vaccinate to inject someone with vaccine. Vaccine is a substance that protects you from getting a certain disease by waking up your body's defenses against that disease.

virus extremely tiny microbe that cannot grow or reproduce by itself, but has to infect a living cell to do so

More Books to Read

Burnie, David, and editorial staff. *Mini Beasts: The Microscopic World of Tiny Creatures.* New York: Dorling Kindersley, 2002.

Favor, Lesli J. *Bacteria.* New York: Rosen Publishing Group, 2003.

Nardo, Don. *Germs.* Farmington Hills, Mich.: Gale Group, 2001.

Rogers, Kirsteen (Editor). *The Usborne Complete Book of the Microscope.* Tulsa, Okla.: EDC Publishing, 1999.

Snedden, Robert. *Microlife: A World of Microorganisms.* Chicago: Heinemann Library, 2000.

Ward, Brian R. *Microscopic Life in Your Home.* North Mankato, Minn.: Smart Apple Media, 2004.

Index